Surviving the Flood

Written by Mary-Anne Creasy

Flying Start
to Literacy®

Contents

Types of floods

A flood happens when there is too much rain in the one place at the one time. There are different types of floods.

Fast floods

Some floods happen quickly. These floods happen when there is sudden, very heavy rain. The water level in rivers and dams rises quickly and the water flows over their banks.

Slow-moving floods

Some floods happen slowly. These floods happen when there is a lot of rain over many days or weeks. The water in rivers and dams rises and overflows. The water can spread into towns and cities. Sometimes, it takes days or even weeks for the slow-moving floodwaters to reach towns.

Flash floods

In towns and cities, drains are built so that rainwater has somewhere to go. If there is very heavy rain and too much water for the drains, the water will flow down the streets. This is a flash flood.

Chapter 1
Before the flood

Monday

On Monday, we heard the news.

Lots of rain had fallen in the mountains near our city. The water was rushing down the river towards us, and we had to prepare for a flood.

The place where we live is warm most
of the time, and we get heavy rain in
summer. Our house is built high off
the ground on stilts so when it does rain,
the water cannot go into our house.

We found out that this flood was going to be different. The floodwaters were going to get high enough to go into our house. We had to prepare for a flood and maybe to leave our house.

The first thing we did was to buy tinned food, candles and bottled water. We didn't know how much time we had or what we should take for safekeeping. We packed up clothes and photos into bags to take with us.

Then we put our furniture and books up high so the water couldn't damage them.

Friends came and helped us move things to their houses, which were on higher ground. One friend took our washing machine, and another took our dining table and chairs.

A man came to our house and turned off the electricity and gas. Water and electricity are dangerous together.

There were cars driving around with loud speakers telling everyone to leave their homes and go to somewhere safe.

Chapter 2
During the flood

Wednesday

Then we saw the brown water slowly creeping up the street towards our house. It was time to leave. We went to a friend's house, which was on high ground and waited.

 We listened to the news on the radio all day and all night. We wondered: How high would the water go? Was it going into our house?

Then we heard some good news. The floodwaters had stopped rising. Our house should be safe!

Thursday, Friday and Saturday

The next morning, we drove as close as we could to our street, which was flooded with water. The water had come up to our floorboards, but not into our house. But we couldn't go back home yet. For three days, we waited for the floodwaters to retreat.

Boats were going up and down the streets instead of cars. Ducks and other water birds were enjoying themselves in the muddy water.

Some houses were almost completely covered by floodwater. We thought we were lucky that our house was built on stilts.

Chapter 3
After the flood

After the floodwater went away, we went back to our house. Our swimming pool was full of muddy water. Under our house, there were boxes of photos and other things we had forgotten about. They were ruined.

Lots of people volunteered to help the flood victims. Strangers came to our house to help us clean and take ruined things away.

We were told to put anything that was ruined outside on the street so it could be collected and taken away. Soon, there were huge piles of rubbish because everyone was throwing away damaged furniture and other muddy objects.

Some of the streets were so thick with mud
that cars could not drive on them.

Two weeks after the flood

It was summer and the electricity was still not on. In the hot weather, food goes bad quickly, so we had to throw away everything in our fridge.

We used candles and torches, and our first meal back in our house was cooked on the barbecue.

Three months later

It took a long time to get our house back to normal. We had to remember who had our washing machine!

We will never forget the flood, and this reminds us to make sure we will be ready next time because the floodwaters might go into our house.

A note from the author

In 2011, my home city of Brisbane, Australia, flooded after months of heavy rain in the mountains nearby. We were warned it was going to be a severe flood, but we did not know what to expect. How high would the water go?

We were lucky. We packed up our house, which is built high off the ground on stilts. But many people were not so lucky and lost everything.

Many photos and other precious items, which we had stored under our house and had forgotten about, were destroyed by the floodwaters. Now, we keep these things inside our house, where hopefully the floodwaters will never reach.